LEARNING LEISURE CONSUMER

PSYCHOLOGY

JOHN LOK

Contents

Preface

Introduction

In global service industry, entertainment industry has high market share in overall industries. entertainment industry may include: hotel, tourism, movie, music, sport, publishing, electronic playing game etc. these main several aspects. Human must need any kinds of entertainment, for example, liking reading people who must go to book stores or enter e-publishing stores to buy any paper books or e-books to read. Otherwise, like sport or enjoyment tourism people, who must choose to spend time to play any football, basketball or swimming etc. different kinds of sports or going to travel agents to pay money to buy air tickets to choose anywhere to travel.

Hence, due to human needs any kinds of entertainment to enjoy our lives, instead of working. If any entertainment businessmen can predict whether what factors will influence general entertainment consumers' entertainment choices change as well as they can predict why and how their entertainment consumption of kinds change. Then, their entertainment businesses can have much accurate prediction to any kinds of entertainment consumers' behaviors.

This book explain some psychological concept to analyze why and how the different kinds of entertainment consumers' entertainment needs how brings economic growth.

Prologue

Table of content

ONE

SPORT INDUSTRY ENTERTAINMENT CONSUMER PSCYHOLOGY

Nowadays, the sports business industry is made up of establishments and the employees of corporations who are primarily concerned with aspects of sports having to do with management, marketing, economics, and finance, amongst other venues. The sports business industry focuses on the sports themselves, as well as the place of sports in society, and the principles that support the sporting industry. The sports business industry is involved in the merger between sports and business, and how these fields work interactively for mutual benefits and profitability.

The sports business industry is interdisciplinary and may involved planning sporting events and effectively marketing for sports, as well as working with accounting, communications, law, and psychology skills. The sports business industry tackles the development of risk management plans for any legal issues that may occur, the negotiations of contracts for players in the industry, and/or strategies for effective media relations.

In fact, instead of sport indutry may include any kinds of sports, e.g. swimming, football, basketball, table tennis, tennis, riding bicycle, climbing, running etc. different kinds of sports to let young and old people enjoy lives. When they play any kinds of sports, they must need to spend some money to any any kinds of sport tools, e.g. swimming pool, table tennis hand tools, bicyle , football, basketball etc. sport useful tools. So, if any one kinds of sport industry can develop in good suitation, then it can influence the sport related useful products sale number because when the sport entertainment player chooses to spend time to play the kind of sport, then the kind of sport sports need be influenced to rise needs. So, if the kind of sport is popular, then the kind of sport product will also influenced to rise needs. So, how to develop the kind of sport in order to attract global sport entertainment players to choose to play the kind of sport, this sport development factor will influence the kind of sport need or innovative development and its related sport products useful tool need increases globally.

- How legalization impacts sports betting economics

A closer look at factors shaping the future of online sports . For example, Americans place $50 billion to $60 billion a year in illegal sports bets, dwarfing the legal $5 billion in Nevada sports betting. This represents a potentially enormous market now that states can decide whether to legalize sports gambling. Although exciting, uncertainties remain that will impact industry size, scale, and opportunity moving forward.The current state of sports gambling. In the immediate US the Supreme Court's decision to overturn the Professional and Amateur Sports Protection Act (PASPA) in May 2018, some states scrambled to pursue a lucrative opportunity independently, without a federal framework in place. Delaware and New Jersey, the plaintiff of the Supreme Court Case (Murphy vs. NCAA), were the first to act and have seen major returns, with more than $385 million a month being wagered in New Jersey alone. Eight states have currently legalized sports gambling, with more to potentially follow in short order as bills are reviewed by state legislatures. These near-term developments will be interesting to watch as sportsbooks lobby for legalization on the state level.The federal government is attempting to secure a wider blanket agreement on the federal level to protect public welfare and the integrity of the game, and generate sufficient tax revenue. The leagues support a federal framework because it can address their interests on a national level. The sportsbooks would prefer legislation that mirrors the way gambling is currently regulated on the state level by the Nevada State Gaming Commission. This situation, like many legalization efforts, is extremely fluid and will change rapidly as the critical uncertainties mentioned below unfold. Depending on the outcome, companies that are able to get in on sports betting could realize a substantial payout.

Hence, global sport entertainment poduct merchants or suppliers, they must need to know how to avoid the illegal sport products can be sold from internet or online channel to enter the kind of sport product market to compete to them illegally any time. Due to ecommerce is popular , so it influences many sport entertainment products consumers may choose to buy any kinds of sport products from online in preference. So, they can not neglect these illegal sport entertainment product sellers' sale behaviors from internet any time.

For US sport industry development example, economists estimate the economic scope of the sports industry in the United States. Drawing on a variety of data sources, they investigate the economic size of sport participation, sports viewing, and the supply and demand side of the sports market in the United States. Estimates of the size of the sports industry based on aggregate demand and aggregate supply range from $44 to $73 billion in 2005. In addition, participation in sports and the opportunity time cost of attending sporting events are important, but hard to value, components of the industry

Sport is a complex, multi-faceted activity encompassing modern spectacles like the Summer and Winter Olympic games and informal pick-up games on urban basketball courts; a recreational jogger, a runner in the Boston Marathon – a competition with thousands of participants -- and people watching the Boston Marathon on television all participate in sport in some way. So, such as Boston Marathon sport game example, if it can provide good sport entertainement show to let global sport auidence to feel exciting and visable enjoyment. Then, the year Boston Marathon competitive game can help advertisement industry and the tennis sport product industry increase tennis products buyer number and advertisement entertainment income and the Boston Marathon competitive game show income. So, one good sport competitive show may help the country's GDP growth, e.g. World Cup football competitive show, World Cup riding competitive show, World Cup swimming show etc. So, any countries government can not neglect how to develop and innovate and promote themselves any sport competive shows and sport entertainments in order to raise GDP growth and create more related sport occupations to reduce unemployment ratio in our nowadays society.

Relatively little attention has been paid in the past to estimating the economic scope of the sports industry, perhaps because of difficulties formulating an appropriate economic definition of sport. A sizable literature documenting the economic scope and economic impact of specific sports or sporting events, already exists, in part because of the ease of defining the limits of events like a golf tournament or season of professional baseball sport industry.

One key issue in defining sport involves identifying criteria that separate sport from games of skill like chess or poker and from recreational activities like dancing, hiking, fishing, and gardening. A secondary issue involves identifying criteria that appropriately define competition in a way to distinguish sport from exercise. For example, running has a competitive dimension but jogging does not. Note that weightlifting is an Olympic sport, bodybuilding is a professional sport, and competitions based on athletic performance on fitness equipment like stationary rowing machines, elliptical trainers and stationary bicycles exist, blurring the already murky distinction between exercise and sport.

In estimating the economic scope of the sports industry is to define the industry in economic terms. Several frameworks for defining the sports industry have been proposed; much of this research emerged from Europe, where government policymakers took an interest in estimating the overall economic importance of sport several decades ago. While a national income and product accounting approach has some appeal, because of the well-developed methodology and the existence of rich set of frequently updated accounts for many developed economies, it also has some weaknesses. First, on the national product side the analyst is at the mercy of the existing production classification system. All levels of government are involved in the provision of sports facilities and other important activities on the supply side of the sports market, and national income and product accounts do not contain detailed estimates of government spending on many specific items. Much of the activity in the sports market involves non-traded goods and labor inputs not valued at market prices, such as WORLD CUP SPORT COMPETITIVE GAME, WORLD GOLF, WOLRD TENNIS SHOW as well as any sport service workers they are needed to work in these any one big shows. Hence, the sport show audience number will influence any one these sport show income and employees number. The sport show employees needing number will depend on these activities factors , such as:

1. Activities involving participation in sport
2. Activities involving attendance at spectator sporting events
3. Activities involving following spectator sporting events through some media.

We recognize that each component contains elements that could be defined as recreation, exercise, or games of skill. For example, including participation in sport means that some activities that could be defined as exercise, like aerobics or walking, will be included in our definition. Including spectator sports means that auto racing, figure skating, and other such activities will be included in our definition.

Individuals can participate in the sport market in three ways: by participating some sport, by attending a sporting event, or by watching or listening to a sporting event on television, radio, or the internet. Each generates direct and indirect economic activity. All three take time, and economic theory tells us that time use has an opportunity cost. In this case, the opportunity cost of individual participation in sport is the value of the next best opportunity for an individual. For consumers of sport, this opportunity cost can be valued in terms of forgone wages or earnings. Furthermore, participating in sport requires equipment, fees, and potentially travel, all of which generate economic activity. Attending a sporting event involves purchasing tickets, travel and perhaps other purchases like food and souvenirs. Watching or listening to sporting events requires equipment, in the form of televisions, radios or computers, as well as subscriptions to broadcast services. Since all of these economic activities increase with the number of participants, documenting the number of participants is an important indicator of the scope of the sports market.

On conclusion, more importantly, individuals' participation in the sports market generates significant economic benefits beyond direct and indirect economic activity. Individuals derive satisfaction, or utility, from participation in the sports market, which has economic value. In economics view, individuals' participation in the sports market produces consumption benefits. These consumption benefits are not bought and sold like tickets, but they are important when assessing the overall scope of the sports market. Although placing a dollar value on sport related consumption benefits is beyond the scope of this paper, it is safe to say that the value of these consumption benefits rises with the number of participants in the sports market.

● Sport consumer behaviors

Despite the recent rapid spread of leisure involvement and loyalty research, very little attention has been given to the conceptualization of the nature of involvement's relationship with loyalty of sport fans. Whether psychological commitment and attitudinal loyalty intervene in the relationship between sport fans' involvement and their behavioral loyalty to a soccer team. For a soccer team sport competition example, it indicate that psychological commitment and attitudinal loyalty intervene in the relationship between sport fans' involvement and their behavioral loyalty to the soccer teams. It is suggested that marketing strategies may be developed to strengthen psychological commitment and attitudinal loyalty in order to maximize behavioral loyalty.

Involvement has been defined as 'a person's perceived relevance of the object based on inherent needs, values, and interests' (Zaichkowsky, 1985, p. 342). Leisure involvement refers to an unobservable state of motivation, arousal or interest toward a recreational activity or associated product that is evoked by a particular or stimulus that possesses drive properties (Iwasaki & Havitz, 1998).

So, any sport competitive show's audience , their psychological commitment factors are very important. They may include: psychological commitment ,attitudinal loyalty behavioral loyalty. For example, psychological commitment is a mediating variable between involvement and behavioral loyalty. Additionally, attitudinal loyalty is a mediating factor that facilitates the relationship between psychological commitment and behavioral loyalty. It seems

that not all highly involved spectators become loyal to their team, although higher levels of enduring involvement seem to be an important precursor to behavioral loyalty. Higher levels of psychological commitment, in which attitudinal loyalty is a crucial element, appear essential for the development of spectators' behavioral loyalty to a team. The development of spectators' behavioral loyalty appears to be best explained as a progressive process in which the formation of high involvement seems to be a precondition for becoming a committed spectator of a team.
On conclusion, any sport competitive shows, how the show can influence and attract audience, the entertainment attractive factor will influence the time sport show success in sport industry long term development. So, how to develop sport entertainment show, it will be one important issue to bring any country's sport income nowadays.

● SPORT HEALTH INFLUENCES SPORT CONSUMERS NUMBER INCREASES

I beleive that when one country is experiencing stable economic growth, it will lead more healthier, I shall indicate reasons as below:
How can economic growth lead healthier to poor people? Can economic growth influence medical service quality and doctors and nurses medical service performance of hospitals? Can economic growth influence quality of medicine to let patients to eat in order to raise more healthier? Has economic growth and medical health service (production of medicine quality) direct or indirect relationship to lead patients more healthier? What are health impact income?
I assume that life expectancy will be better, if the country

has better economic growth or it improves its economic growth. I shall indicate the reasons include as below:
Firstly on relationship hand , I believe that it has relationship between income and health or life expectancy hand, due to the country can develop or grow up or grow its economy to remain long term good economic development. So, its citizen can have more jobs supply to do to treat any sickness. So, they will have effort to buy different kinds of medicine to eat in order to raise more healthier. It seems that some economists support long term good economic growth will bring the country's medical development, e.g. many hospitals can have more effort money to spend to research any new kinds of medicines to let patients to choose the most health medicines to eat, when patietns have different kinds of medicines to choose to eat in order to choose to eat th enough nutrition improvement of different kinds of medicines. Then, the country's patients will have more chance to treat their sickness to be improved health.

Hence, it seems that hospitals will have enough money to research ,when the country has long term better economic growth condition. When the country can remain long term better environment growth improvement, it can lead many jobs to be supplied to people to work and they will have more income to save to buy any expensive medicines, if they are facing serious sickenss, e.g. cancer. Then, they can buy this cancer medicines to eat to treat cancer disease (non common sickness) in order to be more healthier.

Thus, economic growth can lead medical industry has enough money to carry on researching any new kinds of medicines to attempt to treat any serious diseases in order to provide different kinds of new medicines to human to eat to treat any serious diseases more healthier. For example,

U.S., U.K. these both developed countries can remain long term good economic groth. So, these both countries have enough money to assist domestic hospitals to carry on researching any new kinds of medicines to let patients to choose the most effective or more healthier medicines to let patients eat to attempt to treat their serious diseases more successfully. So, U.S., U.K. serious diseases of patients whose death ratio is decreasing in these two countries as well as their death ratio, due to serious diseases causing is the least to compare to other countries.

Secondly, I shall indicate on the improvement in health and economic growth hand, how any why it has relationship between improvement of human health and economic health. I shall focuse in particular on the question of how much of the improvement in health can be attributed. The improvements in the health can include that human's living of standard, better nutrition, changes in the public health environment, it includes sanitation and supply of clean water. Finally an improvement in medical technology, for example, both sanitation improvements and treatment with antibiotics will reduce mortality from infectious diseases.

However, we can explain why economic growth and improvements of human's health , which has relationship. It can be measured by mortality, it can be linked to specific changes in both ages at which people, i.e. an increase age of the number of patients to disease, such as U.S. , U.K. these both countries, the number of old age people who have serious diseases of the total population ratio is less than the developing countries, e.g. China, Africa. It is possible to explain because these both countries have stable long term better economic growth to compare these both developing countries.

Thirdly, I shall indicate on the better nutrition of food supply and economic growth relationship hand. It seems that better economic growth in the country , it will encourage the country people have more consumption effort, then they have enough food to earn more better nutrition to live. So, their diseases will be reduced, due to they have enough food to supply to them to eat to earn more nutrition from different kinds of foods every day, e.g. beef, pork meat, vegetable , fruit etc. food. Hence, economic growth can encourage any food consumers have effort to spend too much expenditure to buy any kinds of fresh and good taste and better nutrition of food to eat. So, it implies the long term stable economic growth will encourage human to buy any kinds of better nutriction of food to eat every day. It can lead human has better healthier, due to human can hace more money to buy better nutriction of food to eat. It includes the special poor people who have effort to buy better nutriction of food to eat.

To sum up, the better nutrition of food is mainly to be consumed by the more effort of the country' poor people when the country have good economic growth environment. So, economic growth can lead any countries' hospitals to research more different kinds of medicines to be attempted to provide to any serious diseases patients to eat. The country's poor people can be raised more healthier to live in the stable economic growth countries.

- Sport industry development brings economic growth

I believe that economic growth must have relationship to influence human development. But it must not lead positive human development. Otherwise, when one country is experiencing stable economic growth in long term. It is possible to lead negative human development. I shall indicate as below:

To explain whether economy growth can influence human development. We need to research whether economy growth has relationship to influence human development. What is economic growth meaning? Economists explain it means an increase in gross national product (GNP) if all products and services that an economy produces during a specified time period. So, it brings one interesting question concerns economic growth: IS it a quantity based concept, not quality based concept? If economic growth is an only relationship to economic development Otherwise, if it also has quality based concepts, then it has relationship to influence or lead human development. When economy growth is a direct measure of changes in the size of the economy. Whether it is a measure of welfare to human development or sustainable development.

Why do we need to concern economic growth? Because political importance means domestic and international trading income and the country's people earning income measurement as well as humanitarian importance means an indicator of welfare, an indicator of human development and an indicator of sustainable development measurement. However, if seems GNP or GDP measures that value of products and services produces within an economy (economic income) in a given year, but it can also measure of welfare development, sustainable anything. Otherwise, human development includes welfare, which measures quality of life and human development, which means quality based concept as well as sustainable income, which means how much we can spend without running down capital stocks, we can maintain same level of spending in perpetuity. Hence, human development concerns our quality of life or standard of living. So, human welfare separation of means from a direct measure of well-being as well as economic welfare separation of means GNP or GDP corrected for expenditures on various necessities. So, it brings this question: Can GDP (economic growth measurement) be an indicator of human development or human welfare? I shall indicate cases to attempt to explain as below:

For GDP per capita and happiness case example, I assume that the country , US increases rapidly up to capita US $4,000 per capita in this year and small returns after that. What does this mean? What influences US people feel happy or happiness feeling causes? For another changing in GDP correlate to changes in environment quality case. Environmental KC (Kuznets Curve) showed the graphical representation of Kuznets theory from the 1940 year that economic inequality increases over time, then at a critical point begins to decrease. Environmental KC (EKC) shows a hypothesized relationship between various indicators of environmental degradation and income per capita.

The EKC (environment Kuznets Curve), shows that in the early stages of economic growth degradation and pollution increase, when beyond some level of income per capita , which varies for different indicators. The trend reverses , so that at high-income levels economic growth leads to environment improvement. This implies that the environment impact is an inverted u-sharped function of income per capita. Thus, EKC implies that economic growth has relationship to influence or lead environmental pollution causing, due to many factories are manufacturing any products during economic growth period. All air or water pollution will increase, due to factories manufacturers manufacture lot of products. The scale effort brings that economic growth increases environmental pollution if there is no change in other factors. The other factors include that change in output mix, change in input mix, state of technology, production efficiency and demand for " improved environment". Hence, when these factors have no change and factories need to use many resources to manufacture lot of products in the manufacturing process. It will bring serious pollution, due to these factories have not improved its technology, production efficiency to avoid to pollute environment to cause local pollutants, deforestation, biodiversity, river low quality, carbon and air low quality, waste increases with increased income. Hence, it is an evidence to explain economic growth will have possible to cause pollution indirectly as well as poor quality of life (standard of living) to influence our life. IT is a good evidence to explain how economic growth can lead human's quality of life (standard of living) to be poor. SO, it brings these questions as below:

Should we always aim to increase GDP? Should we choose to either gain ultimate happiness or either increasing GDP? Is it an indicator of wealth to depend on what GDP really measures? Should we need to concern environment degradation cost or our nervous stress from environmental pollution causing?

In conclusion, it implies that economic growth can lead positive human development , such as economic welfare influence, but it can also lead negative human welfare of long term air or water pollution influence and this challenge can not be solved to any countries in our life if any countries do not attempt to keep balance between achieving economic growth and clean environment in order to not influence our quality of life to be poor. The important evidence , it explain it has relationship between economic growth and human development and they have cause and effect relationship.

- Economic growth leads human employment growth

I believe that when one developed cuntry is experiencing stable economic growth, it can lead human employment growth in high technologic job market, but it can also bring unemployment to low knowledge or skill job, such as cleaning, laboring job market, due to artificial intelligence technology will replace many low skillful job in the future. I shall explain as below:

I assume that it has positive relationship between the accumulation of human capital relation to total employment and GDP growth. It means that a positive relationship between economic growth and the demand for qualified labor are consistent with the hypotheses of the form in the industrial export sector positively influenced by the accumulation of human capital. I shall explain the reason why economic growth can lead positive human employment growth as below:

Namik, (1965) explained that economic growth theories reflect on the continuous increases in the gross national product, because of interaction that occurs in a given environment; in a certain time period, including various changes in the presentation of productive factors in society labor, capital and nature resources to lead these radical changes to increase successive demand on commodities and hence an increase in national income.

Hence, society labor knowledge or skillful development will be one important factor to influence any country's economic growth. If the country has many good educational and skillful labor, then the country will have more possible to raise economic growth for long term, due to they can apply their expertise skills and knowledge to attribute to their country's different kinds of high skillful or knowledge jobs or occupations to do in order to raise themselves country's productivities efficiently. Hence, economic growth has more effort to raise human (labor) these knowledge or skillful development in possible. Considering how economic growth leads labor's skillful and knowledge development positively, I shall indicate these factors as below:

Firstly, on manufacturing industry labors development factor hand, I assume that China's industrial export sector has been positively influenced by the accumulation of human capital , due to many China young people who had graduated any different kinds of degrees, e.g. engineering, education, law, accounting, business, management, chemical , medical , architectural , biology, medicine, computer science, earth science, space science, ocean science, environmental science etc. different kinds of subjects from overseas universities or local universities. Them they apply their expertise knowledge to attribute their skills to do any kinds of professional jobs in China's society. Due to China's sudden economic growth , so it reflects on the continuous increase in the good gross national product, because it occurs in a given good economic environment in a certain time period, due to the global different kinds of China's product number need is increasing as well as many China product manufacturers need many high educational and skillful labors to attribute their effort to help them to develop their businesses in China during the good economic growth period. Hence, China's economic growth leads China's any kinds of product manufacturers who need to employ any kinds of high educational and skillful employees (labors) to do their different kinds of jobs , due to global any kinds of China product consumers' needs are increasing suddenly. Then, it causes the effort to China employees who prefer to spend expenditure to train any young graduated people to be qualified high educational skillful labors with the good conditions of production; which leads to competitive sectors to attract these lacking working experiences of young graduated people t to be the availability of qualified labors in China in order to raise enough employment supply number to satisfy China's manufacturers' labor needs. So, it is a reason to explain that China's high educational and skillful labors development aims to attract foreign investment at a time. The overseas countries seek to provide investment environment through international laws and regulated that only provide qualified labor able to deal with modern technology to China's manufacturing industry development. So, China's economic growth will lead China's knowledge and skillful labors development in possible.

Secondly, on human capital education accumulation factor hand, economic growth will lead human capital educational level to be raised. I shall explain that why economic growth can lead human capital education accumulation positive reason as below:

I shall suppose that the negative impacts in the economic growth rate, it will bring the poor qualified human capital education level. I believe that it has direct relationship between education and the economic growth rate. I shall also suppose that the principle variable of interest determining GDP per capita is the level of labor supply which accounts for all the different educational level, (i.e. primary education, secondary education and university education).

Human capital accumulation can be explained to contribute to utility maximization. In general, it is a direct contribution in the utility function, this is because the more human capital each individual can accumulate in terms of knowledge and skills, the more happiness will be obtained for each one. Hence, it brings this question: Why can economic growth lead human capital accumulation educational level to be raised? The reason is because that when one country has good economic growth, then any primary, secondary and university schools have enough effort or resource to raise teacher individual teaching skills in order to teach many high knowledge and skillful level of students and satisfy their learning needs. Hence, the factors of these primary, secondary and university schools' educational inputs will also be raised, such as the teacher individual characteristics, their educational quality and educational experiences and qualities of their educational services provided and the interest of the country in accumulating educational high level of human capital need. For example, when the country encounters a high economic growth rate, it is able to demand new technology ,as a result of its well-educated society , such as China is one developing country, it needs a well-educated society to educate or train its high educational or skillful labors when it is experiencing in one good economic growth period. So, China's firms encouraged to adopt the advanced technologies developed in high income countries , when global economic growth is coming. It will cause the country, such as China will need to educate many high educational and skillful level labors to do any kinds of high technological jobs in itself country. So, China is a developing country because it needs to develop high technological manufacturing industry, it explains how its economic growth leads high educational and skillful labors development.

Consequently, such as these two cases indicate that one country's economic growth will be possible to lead high educational and skillful labors development in order to raise its competitive ability in different kinds of industries. In specially, high technological development industry , it needs significant high number of educational and skillful labors to satisfy the country's labor market when it is experiencing good economic growth period because many country's high technological product industry is their main income source. So, when the these countries are experiencing good economic growth period, it will lead the human employment growth positive effect for this kind of industry in possible.

● Economic growth leads income inequality

I believe that when one country is experiencing stable economic growth, it will bring serious negative influence to raise income inequality bewteen high education and low education people's income. I shall explain the reasons as below:

Why does the country's economic growth lead negative income inequality influence? Does either the country's high economic growth lead high income inequality or its low economic growth lead low income inequality in appropriate rate? I shall explain that what reasons to lead

income inequality, when the country has high or low economic growth influence as below:
Many economists believed that the relationship of reverse causation from inequality to growth. It has a negative relationship between high economic growth and income inequality. I assume that the gross domestic products per capita to the level of inequality in income distribution. The unequal distribution of income seems similarity to the economic development process.
In fact, the first time , the economic development tends to increase inequality, but the trend is reversed, inequality stabilizes, the decrease until it reaches the lowest level that can be seen in the industrialized economies. So, when the country is encountering farming or agricultural economies or this farming industry won't be easier to lead income inequality. Such as Africa is a farming industry African income level won't have significant income inequality, due to it lacks high technological economic development in itself country and its main jobs are most relate to farming, low technological and low educational need of different kinds of farming jobs. So, the high income and low income people's salaries are not significant difference too much. Otherwise, industrialized economic country, such as China, many Chinese workers are working in different kinds of industrialized jobs in China. However, although, the industrial industry brings economic growth in China society. But, China's high and low income of industrialized workers' wages, they have large significant difference. For example, the computer programmers and computer inventor salaries and the computer manufacturing workers' salaries, they have large significant difference, for another example, the vehicle designer and vehicle inventor salaries and vehicle manufacturing workers' salaries, they

have large significant difference. Due to computer programmer or computer inventor needs have high technical knowledge, but computer manufacturing needs have low technical knowledge as well as vehicle designer or vehicle inventor needs have high vehicle components knowledge to invent any kinds of new styles of vehicles, so their salaries must have high income significant difference to compare the vehicle or computer manufacturing worker. Hence, due to their educational and skillful level is significant difference, so it causes their income will have much significant difference in industrialized industry.

Hence, although China is encountering economic growth, but it also leads high income inequality to China's labors, due to it is one industrialized country. For Africa farming country example, its main industry is agricultural sector, designed as the traditional low-productivity sector in the Africa economy and it can not be replaced easily by the industrial sector. In this traditional farming industry, Africa can not develop its economy to grow up easily. So, it leads its labors' salaries level , which has less or low income inequality causes. Otherwise, such as China is a industrialized industry country, it has different kinds of industrialized development of this sector, such as the computer manufacturing or computer program sector and the vehicle manufacturing and vehicle design invention sector, which produces a movement of labor form low-productivity to high productivity sector, e.g. the vehicle sector is one low number productivity sector and computer sector is one high number productivity sector. This is reflected by an increase in income inequality in China's industrialized society.

Hence, such as above cases, Africa is one farming country, so it causes economic growth is slow and African income level is less inequality. Otherwise, China is one industrialized country, so it causes economic growth is fact and Chinese's income level is more inequality. It can conclude that fast economic growth country will lead high income inequality. Otherwise, slow economic growth country will lead low income inequality.

Banerjee and Newman (1993) indicated a relationship between the choice of occupation and the development process with the presence of an imperfect credit market. In this context, the occupation requiring a high level of investment is undoubtedly devoted to the wealthiest of the population. So, they believed that and industrialized countries will have more occupation choice to let themselves country's people to choose the best salary level of jobs to work. Due to industrialized development causes their economic growth is fact. So, it causes many occupations are created to let themselves country's workers to choose to work, then fast economic growth causes many occupations creating and it leads high income inequality. Otherwise , the farming countries, they have slow economic growth. So, it causes less occupations choice to let themselves people to choose to work and the slow economic growth countries will lead low income inequality.

Consequently, it explains that it has relationship between whether the country is industrialized economy or farming economy or technological economy as well as high economic growth or low economic growth . Then, it has also relationship between high or low economic growth and more or less occupation choices. In final, it has relationship between more or less occupation choices and high and low income inequality. In sum up, high or low economic growth will lead high or low income inequality in possible.

Reference

Iwasaki, Y., & Havitz, M.E. (1998). A path analytic model of the relationship between involvement, psychological commitment and loyalty. Journal of Leisure Research, 19(2), 256-280.

Zaichkowsky, J.L. (1985). Measuring the involvement construct. Journal of Consumer Research, 12(3), 341-352.

TWO

TOURISM AND THE ENTERTAINMENT AGE:THOUGHT ON AN INTERNATIONAL TRAVEL PHENOMENON

Nowadays, tourism entertainment activity is very popular. Every country government must have itself tourism development strategy to seek how to persuade other countries' tourists choose to travel to its country in preference. So, tourism entertainment incomce will be one imporant market share to any countries' overall GDP income. How to excite other countries tourists to choose itself country to travel in preference. It is one interesting question to any countries' tourism policy decision market. I shall indicate some cases concern how to predict and excite travellers' entertainment psychology in order to bring attractive tourism experience to any countries as below:

THE USE OF SOCIAL MEDIA AND ITS IMPACTS ON TRAVELLER BEHAVIOUR

Nowadays, internet is popular to use. Social media enjoy a phenomenal success in terms of adoption and usage levels. They cause every day lives on how people connect and communicate with each other, on how they express and share ideas, and even on how they engage with products, brands, and organizations.Moreover, social media became significant networks of consumer knowledge. In travel and tourism, the impacts of social media have already been described as tremendous, primarily due to the experiential nature of tourism products, and especially of holiday trips: purchases are considered risky and therefore decision making processes are information intensive.

Moreover, social media is all about facilitating people to express and share ideas, thoughts, and opinions with others. It is also about enabling people to connect with others, like they were doing for the last thousands of years. However, what is of significance is that social media: (a) removed spatial and time constrains that were inherent in traditional methods of communications; (b) provided online tools that enable one to many sharing of multimedia content; and (c) employ easy to use interfaces that enable even non-specialists to share and connect. So, any travellers plan to go to anywhere to travel, they will apply internet to attempt to seek any countries' hotel price, air ticket price data as well as seek any countries' destination whether it has anywhere places or locations, they are worth to visit before they decide to go to the country to travel, even they will seek whether the country anywhere have any restaurants to provide the good taste food to them to eat, choosing which kinds of public transportation tools are the most cheapest or the fastest to arrive the destination to travel.

The travellers they will feel to make the accurate expenditure budget before they decide to go to the country to travel when they apply internet to seek any travelling data. Even , some travellers will apply internet media to discuss to other travellers by email media communication channel conveniently.

For example, facebook is the most popular social media networing. During the last years social media are enjoying a phenomenal success: Facebook, a social networking website, many travellers like apply this facebook social media channel to discuss and share their travelling experience together. So, any travellers can apply faccebook social media to know whether the country's any destinations , anywhere are worth to visit or not. Hence, if one traveller had planned to choose the country's some places to travel, but when he feel negative emotion when he discuss with another traveller concerns his past travelling experience to his travelling planning destinaton. Then, he will be influenced to change another country's travelling destination to travel. Hence, facebook media brings the

sudden and rapid travelling plan change to every travellers when they discuss their travelling experience
in their online travelling discuss process.Thus, online social media can bring these several aspects of influences to any gathering data online travellers. They may include as below:

It is one kind social media use and impact during the entire holiday travel process as well as throughout the
holiday travel related consumer decision making processes. It influences during which stages of the holiday travel process to any travellers feel that they need to gather any travelling data from social media before they decide to travel any destination in habit. Hence, online social media can bring impact active users' travel related consumer behaviour in popular.

According to The World Wide Web Consortium (W3C 2004), the web has numerous impacts in
society and culture, science, industry and business: In society and culture the web provides a
new medium of worldwide human communication and revolutionized access to information and
knowledge with implications in all aspects of the daily life from religion and sex to health, politics and commerce. In science, the web has drastically changed the way scientists are doing research: It enables real time access to an enormous amount of information via sophisticated but user-friendly search tools, facilitates cooperation between scientific communities, serves as a new platform for conducting primary research but also as a channel for the dissemination of
scientific knowledge. Due to the web, consumer preferences and the decision making process are not influenced only by the traditionally defined controllable and uncontrollable

stimuli. They are also influenced by the "web experience", or the "online atmospherics" consisting of online controllable factors such as website usability, interactivity, trust, aesthetics, online marketing mix (Constantinides 2004), and by the website's quality, interface, satisfaction and experience (Darley et al. 2010).

On the other hand, there are also signs of negative implications: The Internet and the web makes
consumers highly individualistic, more time driven and demanding, more information intensive,
dictating timing and mode of communication, and with increased expectations (Akehurst 2009).

In addition, the vast amount of information available on the web causes an information overload, impacting negatively on the ability of users to locate information relevant to their needs (Radosevich 1997). Thus, it seems that word wide web or internet invention which can influence travellers feel negative emotion very easy when they apply facebook social media to discuss themselves past travelling experiences. If some travellers often share their negative
travelling experiences to other from facebook social media, when the other travellers read their negative travelling feeling from the words and they will write down on paper to remember
the travelling destinations are not value to attempt to travel.

Then, there are many travelling places are not very attractive to let many travellers to feel when they often share their negative travelling experiences from facebook social media. Although, some travellers want to find the best or the high value of travelling destinations to travel, they shall attempt to discuss or enquire any travellers' opinions from facebook social media. But, in fact, there are many travellers want to find the worst or the less value of travelling destinations from facebook discussion. Hence, facebook social media can influence many travellers' to change their prior destination choices to another later desitnation choices often, when they get the negative travelling experience to share together from the social media internet channel any time.

- Tourism industry element

The tourism industry relies a lot on services and operations; we can classify the operating sector into different hospitality, they may include: accommodation sector, trade trade sector,event sector,attractive sector,entertainment sector, adventure and recreation sector,tourism, transport sector and food sector. Each of the sectors above is different in the services it renders, but sometimes they rely on each other to be more efficient.

The entertainment sector which is the main focus of the research could also be categorized into different segments.These any one service sepect must be important elements to influence overall tourism income and they have close relationship. For example, when one traveller feel the hotel can provide comfortable feeling to satisfy their lving need in his short trip time as well as he can find any entertainment activities easily as well as he can find any cheap and fast public transportation to catch in his trip any time as well as he can find any restaurants to eat good taste food in his whole travelling trip when he visits this country first time. Then, all of these enjoyment and comfortable of travelling feeling will influence he remember this country is one valuable travelling place and he also feels that he ought continue to choose this country to travel again and again. So, if the country can provide the overall travelling activities to satisfy any traveller individual living, eating, transporting and entertainment need. Then, its tourism industry will develop rapidly. For example, theme Parks aims to create an atmosphere of another place and time, and usually concentrates on one dominant theme, around which architecture, landscaping, costumed personnel who are sometimes known as animators, and different facilities for entertainment, distraction, recreation, or physical activities, such as rides, shows, food service and merchandise, are coordinate, because the different facilities in a theme park belong to the same enterprise. (Weiermair,& Mathies, 2007, 228.) Examples are the Walt Disney Magic Kingdom, Disneyland, Sea World Florida, Europe Park Universal Studios and many more. Theme parks are majorly child-friendly, which makes them interesting places for families to visit and they are usually filled with numerous exciting rides, a carnival atmosphere, and several cartoon and movie characters.

On conclusion if any country hopes to develop itself tourism entertainment industry in success
, one country needs to consider many different aspects of entertainment facilities to let travellers to feel fun, excite and comfortable and enjoyable in order to let them can not forget this travelling entertainment activity choice in his/her live. Because any travelling related service elements will have important influence to every first time traveller individual psychology, if the country's any travelling related services can provide the positive emotion to let every traveller to feel. Then, the repeating travellers number will have more chance to increase because they still feel this country can provide the best travelling entertainment service to let them to feel to compare other countries in their life.

● Traveling entertainment industry leads urban environmental planning development need

I beleive that when one country is experiencing stable economic growth, it must lead urban environmental planning development need, I shall indicate reasons as beow:

Can one country's long term stable economic growth lead urban environmental planning development to itself country? Do they have direct or indirect cause and effect relationship between them? I shall indicate some causes to explain whether they have cause and effect relationship between of them existed.

Mexico city is one good example to explain whether itself economic growth has relationship to lead itseld urban environmental planning development recently. Nowadays, Mexico city's economic growth is stable, so it has effort to develop a more livable interlinkage of economic social, and good environmental city to provide to Mexico people to live. It has been developing more livable city by building an efficient intra-urban bus system, expanding urban green space, and meeting the basic needs of the urban poor. Hence, it implies that when one country has long term stable economic growth effort, it is possible that it will plan to develop it's urban environment in order to let its people to live more comfortable, such as Mexico city recent urban environmental planning development core example. So, it explain that why economic growth will bring human's living needs to gain satisfaction in possible.

However, I bring one question: Does it has possible to develop the urban environmental development to achieve the most effective and beneficial to the country's cities , when it had been experiencing the long term stable economic growth period? I shall indiate some evidences to explain this issue whether it can be possible to occur as below:

Every country has thousands of possible sustainable cities, for each city has unique historical , cultural, political and environmental circumstances. Such as U.S. , U.K. these both countries, which have many cities, e.g. Washington, New York, London etc. cities. Every city has unique cultural, historical , political and environmental circumstances backgrounds. So, their urban environmental planning needed to be adapt from approaches formulated in cities and regions, where problems of infrastructure, social equity, and urbanization of the environment have been creatively addresses. They need to know how to design every city's urban to impact on the environment more adapt to make cities more livable for human.

In fact, in economic view point, due to our earth has limited natural resources will continue to provide life support for humanity's lives. So, every country needs to know how to use our earth's limited natural to use our earth's limited natural resources to develop every city's urban environment to let every city's people to live more comfortable to avoid the lacking enough earth's natural resources to be supplied to them to design urban environmental function for every city use in the future one day. Because every country's cities; human population tends to grow, but every country's cities' lands area supply is limited. So, it will cause every city's natural resource is not enough to supply to human to use, when the city's human population growing number has exceeded the city' land area supply to suppot the city's human normal population to live. Hence, it is a value considering question: How to use our earth's natural resource effectively and efficiently and organizing, e.g. land area. It can avoid future natural resource, such as land supply shortage causes human can not satisfy comfortable living environmental need in every cities.

Traditionally, economists have been concerned with the efficiency of resource use. They have been slow in developing economic models that adequately account for resource scarcity and pollution. Only rarely have economists worried that some resources may be short supply, such as clean land and soil , clean water, clear air and theat if these resources are used indiscriminately, they may become exhausted for every city population growth need for which, the city's urban environmental is needed to plan and develop. So, human expected to have comfortable lifestyles.

We need to know how to choose to do our behaviors to avoid environmental pollution, e.g. land, air, water qualities dirty pollution, when the country has long term stable economic growth, it can not neglect how to avoid environmental pollution to every city as the same time. So, when one country has long term stable economic growth. It also needs to plan how to reduce land, air, water natural resources are used by human's wrong attitudes or behaviors to use our earth's natural resources. So, it implies that when one country has long term stable economic growth, it also needs to consider how to plan to develop its urban environment efficiently and effectively and organizing in order to satisfy every city's people's comfortable living needs.

Hence, I bring this question: How to keep stable economic growth and enough natural resources supply to urban environmental development to different countries' cities? I recommend that when every country government needs to encourage businessmen consider environment protection issue when they choose to do and kinds of businesses in themselves countries.

Keating, (1993) explained that how to utilize local materials and are energy-efficient, non-polluting and labor intensive as well as every country government needs to achieve action progress of energy conservation and renewable energy, such as wind, solar, hydro-electric renewable energy, and biomass. For transport policies that favor public, bicycle, and food transport over automobiles municipal development designed to reduce commuting and land use that contains urban sprawl and prevents it from encroaching upon agriculturall land and environmentally sensitive areas are enunciated.

To sum up, in human development history, our earth was relatively empt of human beings and our belongings are only include (man-made capital) and relatively full of other species and our habitats (natural capital). In ago human development history, because human had no any business economic activites. So, human does not need to expand much natural resources to do any business economic activities. Hence, human had enough natural resource to be supplied to use. Till to nowadays, years of economic growth have changed that basic owning enough natural resource supply pattern. As a result, the limiting factor on future encouraging growth has changes. If man-made and natural capital were good substitutes for one another, then natural capital could be totally replaced.

How the two are complementary or however , which means that the short supply of one imposes limits. I shall indicate fishing boats catching fishes to sale business example to explain the economic growth and natural resource shortage relationship issue. If one day, the country's ocean had enough fishing boats to catch fished to sell, but it has without enough population of fishes to be caught to let the fishing boats to catch to sell in the ocean. Once the number of fish sold at market was primarily limited by the number of boats that could be built and manned, not limited by the number of fish in the sea. This suitation is better, due to the natural resources of fishes supply number is enough in the sea. It is only the fish catching boats number is not built enough factor. This cas is similiar to urban environmental development to cities case. When the country had developed long term stable economic growth ,it needs to consider whether human's standard of living is raising up or falling down as the same time. Such as this fishing boats catching fishes business case. If human only consider whether the fishes catching number is increasing every day . But human neglect to consider that one ocean will be polluted and fished will be killed by pollutants. Then, the shortage of different kinds of good taste fishes number challange will cause. Although, human has enough woods or steels resources to build any kinds of fishing boats, but it can't solve fishes shortage challenge. Then, it will lead fishes supply number shortge and it can lead human's living of standard to b fallen down, due to human has no enough fishes to be supplied to eat because many fishes are killed by pollutants in sea. It is similiar to human's urban environmental planning development case. When, human only consider how to remain long term stable economic growth, e.g. building many houses in the limited land area cities, it will damage the city's land green plant and tree growth natural environment as well as the city product manufacturers neglect to avoid to pollute river, air and ocean in their factories manufacturing process. Then , in long term time, when our natural environment is polluted.

Any cities will have only polluted dirty air to human to breathe and dirty water to provide to human to drink and any cities lack enough green and clean soil to grow trees and plants to let human to live comfortable in different cities. Then, human's standard of living or quality of life will be fallen down. So, human ought consider economic growth will lead natural resources number to be decreased as well as environmental pollution challenge causes, due to human's economic action lead this challenge causes.

Consequently, economic growth has possible to lead urban environment planning development needs, due to human had polluted our natural environment and consume the exceed number of natural resource to cause any vegetable and fish and food supply number to be reduced in long term stable economic growth period to every country's economic development. To avoid human needs to reorganize cities and urban environmental development need. Huaman must need to find solutions to avoid to cause serious pollution to our land, sea and river and air in our long term stable economic growth period.

In conclusion, when one country is experiencing stable economic growth , it can perform better economic development. But, it can not absolute perform better human development. Due to human only considers how to do any business behavior to damage our natural environment and misuse our natural resource. Otherwise, when one country is not experiencing stable economic growth, it is possible to lead human development. Due to it's economic development stage is not reach the maximum period. So, the country won't do business behavior to damage its natural environment and misuse natural resource to cause itself people's standard of living to be worse.

reference

Akehurst, G., 2009. User generated content: the use of blogs for tourism organisations and tourism consumers. Service Business, 3 (1), 51-61.

Constantinides, E., 2004. Influencing the online consumer's behavior: The web experience. Internet Research, 14 (2), 111-126.

Darley, W. K., Blankson, C. and Luethge, D. J., 2010. Toward an integrated framework for online consumer behavior and decision making process: A review. Psychology & Marketing, 27 (2), 94-116.

Radosevich, L., 1997. Fixing Web-site Usability. InfoWorld, 19 (50), 81-82.

Weierman K, Mathies C, 2007, The tourism and leisure industry, shaping the future, Binghamton, Haworth press

World Wide Web Consortium (W3C), 2004. W3C 10th Anniversary [online]. Cambridge, MA: World Wide Web Consortium. Available from: http://www.w3.org/2004/Talks/w3c10-Overview/ [Accessed 12 December 2009].

THREE

THE READER'S READING METHOD CHOICE PSYCHOLOGY

It is one interesting question to predict and measure why the reader chooses the book to study or how his /her reading habit behavior or

reading attitude which can influence her/his reading interest or reading book choice in this book sale market. I shall indicate some factors why and how influences reader individual reading behavior or book choice as below:

- Fair Pricing of The eBook or paperBook Perception Factor

Internet can influence buyer choice,such as whether the reader either choose to buy the ebook or paperbook choice .People will pay for convenience, entertainment, art, education, enlightenment, fun, the ability to have something instantly and many will even

pay a little more for a product that is friendly to the environment. In reading industry, ebooks are all of that and they can be read again and again

without costing readers more. People love to be entertained. They love to be enlightened. They love convenience. They love instant gratification.

So why is it that publishers are fighting a pricing battle for ebooks? For example, Amazon wants to see ebooks at $9.99 or less, publishers are fined for allegedly trying to price fix ebooks and readers demand to know why they should have to pay the same for an ebook as they do a paper book.

With authors, publishers, booksellers and consumers all trying to be heard on this topic of ebook prices the question persists; how much should ebooks cost?

In the economic "supply and demand" view, what cost to readers and to the publishing industry? Reading the flurry of articles written about

the DOJ's charges of price-fixing, as a reader, I initially felt like I was being taken advantage of. I must be, because the DOJ is forcing publishers to pay

back some of the money readers paid for books. So obviously readers were over-charged, right? Not necessarily. And I realize that the charges against the publishers are about the conspiracy and not a reflection of what the government thinks ebooks should cost.

Regardless of what it costs to create a book, if no one is willing to pay the price publishers are asking then one of two things will happen; either publishers will offer less books, taking less chances on new authors, or publishers will have to cut costs in other ways to lower pricing. Or, perhaps, publishing houses are no longer needed. So, ebook publishers can replace paperbook publishers more easily if ebook price can keep very low to compare any one paper book price. Of course, a lot of people are speculating to benefit from self-publishing or are struggling to be part of an industry that can't afford them.

When publishers cut costs in order to meet the demands of readers for less expensive books, then the publishers can't take chances on publishing books that are not a sure bet to make money, leaving many out of work authors to move to self-publishing, setting lower prices that publishers are then expected match, which causes them to make less money from epublish online sale channel.

What does this have to do with ebook pricing? A lot really, because it causes us to focus on the side effect of the problem instead of the problem itself.

The problem is that no one is addressing the psychology of fair pricing of ebooks from the point of view of the end consumer; the reader.

Self-published authors are setting their own prices, often starting at $1.99. There are a lot of valid reasons to do this. The author may be looking to gain new readers by selling their back list, their previously published books in which the rights to the book have reverted back to the author, which is a good idea,

or the author may just be looking to make money by selling high quantities of books. Some authors are new and keep the prices low knowing many readers are more likely to purchase a book from an author they are unfamiliar with if the price is low enough. But, big publishers and authors,who have been serially rejected by publishers over the last few years, and are happy to hear the message of antiquated publishers in New York frightened of the future and how those publishers will one day regret rejecting the author.He is also an influencer. Recall that his site did not display a button for books that cost more than $9.99.

On the other hand, readers see the $9.99-or-less message in many places on the internet. Amazon favors the $9.99 price even when it means
they will take a loss selling at that price. They do that as a business strategy to put other booksellers at a disadvantage and in some cases to put them out of business. And though most everyone in the industry knows of this practice and what its intent is, the government chose to see publishers as price-fixing when Apple and several New York publishers got together to discuss how to combat the effects of Amazon's pricing tactics and try to figure
out how to take back their right to publish books at the prices they feel is fair.

Hence paper book publishers will face competition from ebook publishers because their prices are often lower than their general prices when they are displayed on an book shops.
What is a fair price for an ebook? How is that determined? It is determined by a lot of factors.
How much does it cost to create the ebook? How much is a reader willing to pay?

The problem is that publishers have not done one aspect of their job correctly. Yes, publishers do a lot of great things and they do it very well,
but the one thing they should have excelled at, the failed at, and they are now paying the price for it. They have done nothing to create a psychology
of fair pricing within the reader that matches the price they want to get for a book.

Publishers should be working on campaigns that promote books in ways that people are made to understand that a price of $15 – $25 for an ebook is a fair price. They should promote books so that people don't second guess what a fair price is. Do publishers not recognize the issues readers have with ebook pricing? Are they so focused on Amazon that they don't see the needs of their customers? However, paper books still have its attraction ,such as they can be sold, such as second hand book, when the book original buyer does not want to read the book, then he can sell cheaper price more easily. Otherwise, ebook can not resell to anyone in success because they are only read from internet channel. So, if the paper book is more attractive on reading and its price is reasonable, then I believe that it can still attract many readers to choose to buy it to read from book shop because readers believe it can be sold more easily.

Some points to make about ebook prices compared to paper book prices-People tend to think that having an actual, physical book in their hands,

one they can share, re-sell, put on their coffee table and mark on (yes people do mark in their books), are all reasons why they are paying a higher price for a book.

Those are all good reasons, too. We will infer, for the sake of this lengthy article, that people include "good story" and "known author" as part of their acceptance to paying more. The issue seems to be that people feel an ebook has less value because you can't do those things with it. That is simply not the case. In fact, it's not paper and harder to display on your coffee table and you can't re-sell it or even share it as easily as you can a physical book but

you're paying for something of equal value in the trade-off. You don't have to cart around heavy books everywhere you go. You can have instant gratification because you can buy the book and start reading it immediately from the comfort

of your own home.
It is friendly to the environment. It is convenient, given that many books are available across platforms including your computer,
mobile device and/or tablet as well as in some kind of cloud system. So if you forget your ereader at home, but have your mobile phone, you can still read your book.

On conclusion, there are things a reader can do with a physical, paper book that cannot be done with an ebook. There are things a reader
can do with an ebook that cannot be done with a paper book. The reader is paying for preference. They are paying for what they want, how they want it. Where does that de-value ebooks in the mind of readers? That is the big question, isn't it?
Because it is easy to access a book online readers sometimes think ease, less valuable. But that's not true at all.

Ebook reading will become one kind of reading habit from mobile or laptop when the reader leaves his home in any time. Most readers will pay extra for life to be made easier for them. That's why there's valet parking and beauty salons. Yes, we can do those things ourselves, but we pay a lot of money each year to have other people do those things for us. Why? Because it's easier on us. So, ebook reading can let readers go to anywhere to read from their mobile or laptop. It is one kind of attractive new technological reading or learning behavior nowadays.

On conclusion, ebook reading habit will be replaced to traditional paper book reading habit in possible. Perspective is hard to change, especially once someone takes the lead and begins to create expectations. It is up to the publishing industry as a whole to band together and change the perspective of the reader when it comes to

ebook pricing.
Hence, if paper book publishers hope to win their ebook publishers, they need to charge the reasonable book market price, it can not rise highly to compare its similar ebook topic, because when one ebook reader discover one ebook price is very low to compare one paper book, they
have similar contents and topic , then he will prefer buy the similar topic and content ebook to read as well as the paper book must need
to design photo to attract readers' reading interest and price is more reasonable in the paper book sale market. When he read the paper book
long time, he feel bore to read, then he believe that he can sell this paper book (seond hand book) to anyone in less discount price more easily.
When this both factors can achieve that the paper book will also be sold to anyone more easily.

- Electronic Publishing industry brings
knowledge-based economic society

I believe that when one country is experiencing stable economic growth, it can raise knowledge -based economic society, I shall indicate reasons as below:
I shall explain why and how economic growth can raise the country to become one knowledge-based economic society. Knowledge investment means that knowledge distribution is through formal and informal networks, which is essential to economic performance, knowledge -based economies which are directly based on the production, distribution and use of knowledge and information. Knowledge is increasingly being codified and transmitted through computer an communications networks in the information societ. For example, the developed countries, e.g. U.S., U.K. . They have long term stable economic growth

for may years. So, they had been experiencing the knowledge-based economic developed social coutries. Their knowledge-based economic societies will provide them the enabling organizational change at the U.S., U.K. firm level to maximize the benefits to them in both manufacturing and service technology for producing sectors.

The effect of "knowledge"-based economy, which will led a fuller recognition of the role of knowledge and technology in economic growth (human technologial capital) growth to assist or encourage human development. For example, the exports of high technology industries had grown fastly for these knowledge of economic growth developed countries, e.g. Canada, U.S. , U.K. , Australia, Japan, New Zealand, Europe etc. developed countries.

Knowledge-based economic development can also lead more intangible investments in research and development, training of the labor force, computer software and technical expertise to those above countries. So, knowledge-based economic development can lead human's talent development to create new talent human's knowledge to different technological development aspects, e.g. internet invention, 3 D printer invention, advanced medical equipment invention, space boats, nuclear energy invention, prior speed railway transportation tool invention etc. technological products. So, any one of high technological products invention which must need have good economic growth to the country, then when the country has good economic growth condition,it will have effort to train or educate talent human to attribute to knowledge -based societies to encourage or give these chance to talent human or inventors to invent any kinds of high technological products for human to use. Hence, when one country can have effort to be developed to one knowledge-based economic developed country. Then, it can have possible to provide high technological resources to educate or train " talent" humans or scientific inventors to invent any new kinds of high technological products to provide to human to use. So, in the future, oue standard of living will be improved in possible, due to economic growth causes any kinds of high technological products to be invented to provide human to use.

However, I bring this question: Can economic growth bring knowledge-based economic society to lead talent human development really? I shall indicate reasons to explain whether they have relationship to lead talent human development as below:

When the country has good economic growth , employers need skilled labor number will increase in the highest demand. Although, the manufacturing sector is losing jobs, but employment is growing in high-technology, science-based sectors ranging from computers to pharmaceuticals, high knowledge-based jobs. These jobs are more highly skilled and pay higher wages than those in low technology sectors, e.g. textiles and food processing. Moreover, knowledge-based jobs in service sectors are also growing strongly. Indeed, non-production or knowledge-based job in service sectors engage in the output of physical products are the employees in most demand in a wide range of activities from computer technicians, through physical therapists to marketing specialists. The use of new technologies, which are the engine of long -term gains in productivity and employment. Generally improve the " skills base" of the labor force in both manufacturing and services. And it is largely balance of technology that employers now pay more for knowledge than for manual work. So, it seems that economic growth will have possible

to cause knowledge-based economic society to any countries.
Then, I shall explain the question: Can knowledge-based economic society lead talent human development? In fact, it is not a new idea that knowledg plays an important role in the economy . Also economists are now developing new growth theories to explain the forces which drive long-term economic growth. In new growth theory, knowledge can raise the returns on invetment, which can contribute to the accumulation of knowledge. It is done by stimulating more efficient methods of production organization as well as new and improved products and services. Knowledge can also spill over from one firm or industry to another with new ideas used repeatedly at little extra cost. Such spillovers can ease the constraints placed on growth by scarcity of capital.

Hence, it seems knowledge-based economic society will encourage employers to train talent human to contribute their any new kinds of knowledge to do any kinds of new creating jobs. Moreover, knowledge-based economy can also encourage employers to create more different kinds of new knowledge jobs to lead talent human development.
The talent human development includes these complex-areas of knowledge in order to fulfil their jobs as below:
For example, practitioners of law and medicine belong to know-who , it refers to knowledge about " facts ". This knowledge is close to what is normally called information. Know-why refers to scientific knowledge of the principles and laws of nature. It means technological development and product and process advances in most industries, e.g. research laboratories and universities organizations. So, firms need to interact with these organizations either through recruiting scientifically -trained labor or directly

through contracts and joint activities. Know-how refers to skills or the capability to do something. A new product or a personnel manger neede to select and train staff have to use their know-how.

One of the most important reasons for the formation of industrial networks is the need for firms to be able to share and combine elements of know-how. Finally, this is why know-who because increasingly important. Know-who involves information about who knows what and who knows how to do what. It is possible that any talent human expects he.she knows how to use whose knowledge efficiently. The know-who kind of knowledge is internal to the organization to a higher degree than any other kind of knowledges. It is significant in economics, skills are widely disposed because of a highly developed division of labor among organization and experts. For example, for a modern manager who must need to own this kind of knowledge to manage whose organization efficiently and effectively in order to achieve the most maximum beneficial to productivities and raising employee individual working performance.

In conclusion, it seems that it explains why the knowledge-based economic country's employers need to spend expenditure to train talent humans in order to raise their different aspects of knowledge development, when the country is experiencing " knowledge-based economic society".

FOUR

SOFTWARE ENTERTAINMENT GAME CONSUMER BEHAVIOR

How information technologic game strategy influences game player entertainment psychology? How and why information technological game strategy can influence economic growth? I shall explain as below:
Nowadays, Macrosoft and Microcorp are the global information technological big companies. They own much market share in global information technological industry. Whether what factors influence they can still be global information technological products leaders. Why does computer software consumers still choose their products to compare other software products in preference? I suppose that Macrosoft and Microcorp, their hypothetical any software games have developed a clever new computer

game that is certain to be very popular. Although Microcorp have the unique competitive advantage with its own software game engineers and compete against Macrosoft, but it can so it cheaper and better if it can hire any Macrosoft's software game engineers. So, in economic view, it needs to pay high salary (higher cost) to hire Macrosoft's engineers (labor), but Macrosoft's engineers can help Microcorp to invent any new kinds of software games to compete Macrosoft. Although, Microsorp needs to pay higher labor cost, but when it can raise its any software games' design and game playing methods to attract any game players. Then, these new and exciting software games can help it can bring many game entertainment players and then it can sell cheaper price to raise more attractive effort to win its competitor (Macrosoft). So, higher software game designing engineers (skill labor), their game designing effort will be the major factor to influence any one information technological companies in success. If one software designing company can employ one high software game designing effort profession to help it to design any kinds of attractive software games. Although, it may pay high salary (labor cost), but it have much chance to attract many software game buyers to compare that if it pays less salary to employ one poor game software designing profession. Because the poor software game designing profession may need to spend long time to research how to design any kinds of attractive game software to excite game players' playing desires in this playing software game industry market. Long time research to the poor software game designer may be one none any reward to compensate to the software game designing firm when it needs to pay long time salary to employ him. Otherwise, if the software game designing firm can accept to pay higher salary to the higher software game designer, he will have higher chance to help it to design any more attractive software games to influence game players' playing game entertainment desires. So, any software game designing companies their game designers (labor) must be the major factor to influence their business succeeds or fails in this software game entertainment market.

On the employing method hand, Microcorp can choose to include in its contracts with its software engineers that from working for another Macrosoft software company for a certain period of time if they resign from Macrosoft. A move such as this is sometimes called a preeptive move. Its propose is to alter its rivals' payoffs in order to alter their employing strategies. Preemptive moves are usually costly (high slaary), and this one is no exception. In its employment contracts makes Macrosoft a less attractive to let its old game software engineers want to leave their current employer, such as Macrosoft. As a result, Macrosoft must pay its software game designing engineers above the going market salary if it hopes their employment contracts can be continue between Macrosoft and its software game engineers.

Should Macrosoft must need to decide how to react. It can choose to fight Microcorp by aggressively advertising its game, which is costly high, but gives it a larger market share in the game player entertainment market, when Macrosoft had any one profession game software engineer(s) leave(s) his company and he/they change(s) to the another Microcorp software game designing company to work, or it can forego the expense of an advertisement campaign and simply share the market 50/50 with its major competitor, Microcorp to be partners.

Their competition has close relationship to influence

economic growth because it will have many game players number to be increase if they can cooperate to be partners in success when they can design any new kinds of software game products to satisfy software game players' entertainment feeling. Otherwise, if they can not be one good partners and they only consider their every business benefits and neglect themselves business benefits. Then, their software playing games sale price can either to be reduced in order to attract any software game players when their software games can not be designed to have much new playing methods to attract many game players. Consequently, the GDP income to this software game entertainment market must reduce because any kinds of entertainment software games prices are reduced as well as the game players number is also decreasing. Due to they are the major software entertainment game suppliers in global. Any game players will only choose either Microcorp or Macrosoft to buy their any kinds of entertainment software game products to play majorly. So, their software game manufacturing and sale number must influence global GDP income increases or decreases in macro economy view. It implies that any countries technological software game industry's GDP income will depend on these both Microcorp and Macrosoft software game's cooperation relationship whether they have good or bad cooperation relationship. If their cooperation relationship is good, then they can manufacture high quality and attractive entertainment software games as well as raising sale price and exciting many game players' entertainment desires to achieve the increase to game players number aim more easily.

How to achieve their cooperation relationship more easier. I suppose that, in the software game entertainment industry, over its lifetime, the computer game will generate $500,000 in new income (income minus production cost) for all the firms producing it or its clones. Macrosoft must pay its software engineers an additional $100,000 to get them to agree to accept a contract containing an anticompetition clause. It costs Microcorp $100,000 to develop the software if it can hire Macrosoft's engineers and $200,000 otherwise. Aggressive advertising costs Macrosoft $70,000 and has the effect of giving it a 80% market share if it restricts its engineers' employment and a 72% market share if it does not. So, the fall in total market share is caused by the fact that without some of Macrosoft's advertisements. If however, Macrosoft passively acquiesces to Microcorp's entry and shares the market, then both firms can still achieve a 50% market share fairly. Hence, they must need to achieve 50/50 market share if they hope to achieve the cooperation relationship in success. Otherwise, they will not achieve cooperation relationship in success.

However, the spending advertisement factor will also their cooperation chance in success. For example, it would be more realistic to recast the Software Game as one in which Macrosoft chooses how much to spend on advertising with sales depending continuously on the amount spent. Other examples of continuous cooperation choices may include: the productive capacity of an electrical power plant; the salary to offer a prospective employee; or the insurance premium to charge a prospective policyholder. So, the amount to any of these expenditure factor will influence whether they will decide to cooperate to sell their software games products in global game entertainment market.

How and why Macrosoft and Microcorp's cooperation can influence global economic growth? It is significant that Macrosoft and Microcorp both technological software game designing companies are global the largest firms, they are doing international software game trade business to many countries and they have large market share in the software entertainment game sale market. Aside from trade based on technological gaps and software game product cycles, software game entertainment industry is dynamic in nature or game players' entertainment taste will change any time in completely static in nature. That is, given the nation's game players' playing taste and game entertainment factor, such as game playing designing technological method and game player individual playing game taste both. We proceeded to determine the nation's comparative advantage and the gains from the different kinds of entertainment software game designing supply factor and the game player individual game taste changing factor. So, any nation's software game players number will depend on these both factors to influence whether their number will either increase or decrease in the year in this global software game entertainment market. However, these factors can be changed by time, technology usually can improve any software game playing methods and game player individual playing taste will also change any time. As a result, the nation's comparative advantage also changes over time, such as when the nation has many game players lose their interest to buy any software games to play, then the nation ought not only consider how to develop its software entertainment game in the technological industry, it is right time to research any other new technological industries to develop if it still hopes its GDP income can rise in the technological industry overall aspect. Such as dynamic trade theory is still in its infancy. However, our comparative statics analysis can carry us a long way in analyzing the effect on international trade resulting from changes in factor technology, and tastes over time, such as entertainment software game case.

The growth of factors of production will also influence the software game entertainment industry development, through time, a nation's population usually grows and with its size of its labor force , such as China and India. Similarly, by utilizing part of its resources to produce capital equipment, e.g. India needs to utilize its technological resources, technological engineers and technological material can need to be used to manufacture either new software game products or computers. But, its technological resources will be shortage (both labor and technological material). So, many technological companies choose to apply more technological material and technological engineers to use much time and money to manufacture any new software game products. Then, these labor and material resources will be reduced to be spent time and material to manufacture any new computer products in the year. In this technological industry case, capital refers to all the man-made means of production, such as machinery, factories, communication and education and training of labor force, all of which greatly enhance the nation's ability to produce either computer products or software game products. So, the national will also continue to assume that it can experiencing economic growth is producing two commodities, such as software game and computer both kinds of technological products under the constant returns to scale. So, if India can not raise the rapid technical process to skill labor and supply technological material supplying number to satisfy to manufacture the enough software game and computer products to supply them to sell to any countries' playing game players and computer users every month. Then, its

technological industry will lose many clients, due to it can not supply enough software games and computers number to sell to any countries.
Several empirical studies have indicated that most the increase in real per capita income in technological industrial nations is due to technical progress and much less to capital accumulation. However, the analysis of technical progress is much more complex than the analysis of factor growth because there are several definitions and types of technical progress, and they can take place at different rates in the production of either or both commodities, such as software game and computer.
Technical progress is usually classified into neutral, labor saving , or capital saving. All technical progress , regardless of its types reduces the amount of both labor and capital required to produce any given level of output. So, if India could have good technical progress to raise its technological labor skill and reducing the technological material to be used to manufacture the software games and computers. Then, it will have chance to keep the maximum manufacturing level number to software game and computer products as the same time.
On conclusion, it is only Macrosoft and Microcorp's cooperation relationship can influence their any kinds of entertainment game products' playing qualities and entertainment taste to let game players feel more fun and exciting beacase when these both big high technological entertainment game designers like to attempt to cooperate to manufacture their any new kinds of entertainment game products to let children or young people to play in order to satisfy their exciting and actual enjoyment entertainment feeling when they can feel to be the actual person to participate to any game image environment influentically.

Because their cooperation relationship can improve their game paying qualities and raise entertainment enjoyment performance more easily than the their competive relationship in this entertainment game market.

Reference

Banerjee, A. Newman, A. (1993). Occupational choice and the process of development . Journal of political economy, 101 (2). 274-298.

Keating, M. (1993). The earth summit's agenda for change. Geneva: centre for our common future, viii, x, 12-13. 63-67.

Namik, S.D. (1965). The theories of economic growth, Cario: Knowledge House.

9 798887 497167

Printed by Libri Plureos GmbH in Hamburg,
Germany